Energy Essentials

Energy Transfers

Media Center

EXPRESS EDITION

Nigel Saunders and Steven Chapman

Raintree

For information, address the publisher:
Raintree, 100 N. LaSalle, Suite 1200, Chicago, IL 60602

Printed and bound in China
10 09 08 07 06
10 9 8 7 6 5 4 3 2 1

Library of Congress Cataloging-in-Publication Data

Saunders, N. (Nigel)
    Energy transfers / Nigel Saunders and Steven Chapman.
        p. cm. -- (Energy essentials)
    Includes bibliographical references and index.
    ISBN 1-4109-1695-2 (lib. bg. : alk. paper) --
    ISBN 1-4109-1700-2 (pbk. : alk. paper)
    1. Energy transfer--Juvenile literature. 2. Power resources--Juvenile literature. I. Chapman, Steven. II. Title.
    III. Series: Saunders, N. (Nigel). Energy essentials.
    QC73.8.E53S38 2005
    531'.68--dc22
                                    2005003829

This leveled text is a version of Freestyle: Energy Essentials: Energy Transfers.

Acknowledgments

p.4/5, Corbis; p.4, Tudor Photography; p.5, Corbis; p.6, Alamy Images; p.7, (top) Corbis; p.7,(bottom) Getty Images; p.8, (left) Corbis; p.8, (right) Corbis; p.9, Corbis; p.10, Topham Picturepoint; p.11, (top) Science Photo Library; p.11, (bottom) Corbis; p.12–13, Tudor Photography; p.12, Corbis; p.13, Alamy Images; pp.14/15, Trevor Clifford; p.15, Science Photo Library; p.16, (top) Corbis; p.16, (bottom) Science Photo Library; p.17, Corbis; pp.18/19, Science Photo Library/ Martin Bond; p.18, Science Photo Library; p.19, Alamy Images; pp.20–21, Photodisc; p.20, Science Photo Library; p.21, Science Photo Library; p.22, Alamy Images; p.23, Corbis; p.24, Alamy Images; p.25, Getty Images/ Stone; p.26, Corbis; p.27, Corbis; pp.28/29, Corbis; p.28, Getty Images; p.29, Alamy Images; pp.30/31, Science Photo Library; p.30, Corbis; p.32, Science Photo Library; p.33, (top) Nature Picture Library; p.33, (bottom) Science Photo Library; p.34, Science Photo Library/ Rosenfeld Images Ltd; p.35, Alamy Images; p.36, Corbis; p.37, Alamy Images; p.38, (top) Science Photo Library; p.38, (bottom) Corbis; p.39, Science Photo Library; p.40, (right) p.40, (left) Science Photo Library; Corbis; p.41, Corbis; pp.42/43, Science Photo Library; p.42, Alamy Images; p.43, Science Photo Library; pp.44/45, Science Photo Library.

Cover photograph of light bulb reproduced with permission of Getty Images/Taxi

Contents

Any words appearing in the text in bold, **like this**, are explained in the Glossary. You can also look for them in the Word Store at the bottom of each page.

Types of Energy

Energy is being able to do work. It is energy that lets you get up in the morning, get dressed, and walk to school. We can see light energy, we can feel heat energy, and we can hear sound energy.

Energy can be stored as **chemical energy**. A battery is a store of chemical energy. Things that are moving, such as your bike or skateboard, have movement or **kinetic energy**.

Energy in food

Food contains stored chemical energy. Some foods contain more energy than others. A bar of chocolate has more chemical energy than a head of lettuce.

energy   being able to do work. Light, heat, and electricity are types of energy.

Energy transfers

The important thing to remember about energy is that it cannot be made or destroyed. However, it can be changed from one type of energy to another. A firework changes stored chemical energy into heat, light, and movement energy. This energy change is called an energy transfer.

Find out later ...

. . . how energy changes in a roller coaster.

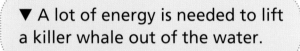

▼ A lot of energy is needed to lift a killer whale out of the water.

. . . why firefighters wear shiny suits.

. . . what submarines and bats have in common.

chemical energy   energy that is released during chemical reactions

Storing Energy

If you pull the two ends of a rubber band apart, the rubber stretches and the band gets longer. When you let it go, the band returns to its starting length. The rubber band stores **energy** when you stretch it and gives it out when you let go. This type of stored energy is called **elastic energy**.

Elastic energy

When an archer (right) pulls back on the string of the bow, elastic energy is stored in the bow. When the archer lets go, the bow goes back to its normal shape. The stored elastic energy is changed into kinetic energy in the arrow.

Word Store   elastic energy   energy stored when something is stretched, squashed, or bent

Bouncing high

A trampoline is made from stretchy material attached to a frame by springs. These springs can store elastic energy. When you jump on a trampoline, your **kinetic energy** is turned into elastic energy in the springs. Each time you bounce back upward, the elastic energy is turned back into kinetic energy.

▲ Stored elastic energy helps you bounce high on a trampoline.

Shock absorbers

Shock absorbers on cars and bicycles (above) make journeys more comfortable. They absorb some of the kinetic energy of the wheels moving up and down over bumps.

kinetic energy   energy of moving things

Gravity

Gravity is an invisible **force** that pulls objects toward the center of Earth. When you jump off a wall, you are pulled to the ground by gravity. **Gravitational energy** is another form of stored **energy**. The heavier an object is and the higher it is lifted, the more gravitational energy it has.

Clockwork

Some clocks, such as the one below, use a pendulum to keep time. A pendulum is a weight that hangs from the center of the clock. As it swings, gravitational energy is turned into kinetic energy and then back again.

▼ A roller coaster changes stored gravitational energy into moving kinetic energy.

Water power

When water is high up, it has stored gravitational energy. In a waterfall, this energy is changed into **kinetic energy** as the water drops. **Hydroelectric power** stations use the power of moving water to turn **turbines** that generate electricity.

Waterwheels

The kinetic energy in falling water makes a waterwheel (below) turn. The energy is transferred from the falling water into the waterwheel. This energy can then be used to turn a millstone or to generate electricity.

hydroelectric power   electricity made by using moving water

Flywheels

When a carousel spins around, it has a lot of stored **kinetic energy**. That is why it is hard to stop it quickly. A **flywheel** is a heavy metal spinning wheel that has kinetic **energy** in the same way. This energy can be changed into other types of useful energy by engines and machines.

The first flywheels had a heavy **rim** that was held in place by spokes—a bit like a bicycle wheel.

Early engines
This steam engine (right) was built in 1804. It has a huge flywheel.

Car engines

A car engine has three or more **cylinders** in its engine. They are joined to a spinning rod and move up and down. A flywheel keeps the engine turning between the power strokes from the pistons. This smoothes the engine's movement.

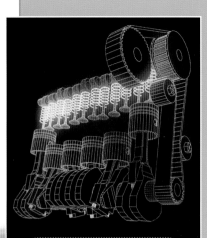

▲ The cylinders in an engine move up and down.

◀ A spinning playground merry-go-round has a lot of kinetic energy, just like a flywheel.

Chemical Energy

Everything around us is made up of tiny **particles** called **atoms**. Atoms are joined by chemical **bonds** to make many other substances. When a **chemical reaction** happens, some bonds are broken and new bonds are formed. When this happens, **energy** is sometimes released.

Some substances are useful stores of **chemical energy**. They release a lot of energy when they take part in chemical reactions.

▼ Batteries come in all shapes and sizes.

The first battery

The first battery was made in 1799 by an Italian scientist named Alessandro Volta. He used a tall stack of zinc and copper discs (above). Volta's battery was large and difficult to use.

Word store   atom   smallest bit of a substance

Batteries

A battery is a store of chemical energy. This chemical energy in the battery is turned into electrical energy when the battery is switched on. Batteries provide electrical power for things like torches, cameras, and cellular phones.

Rechargeable batteries

Most batteries have to be thrown away when they run out. However, rechargeable batteries can be used over and over again. They are recharged by putting electricity back into them. This electric car (above) has rechargeable batteries.

Energy graph

Some types of food are better stores of energy than others. Our bodies can use all the energy in carbohydrates and nearly all the energy in fats. But they cannot use all the energy in proteins. This graph shows how much energy, in **joules**, we can get from each type of food.

Energy in food

Food contains stored **energy** that our bodies can use. Food groups include carbohydrates (such as potatoes and pasta), fats (such as milk and butter), and proteins (such as meat). Other things, such as vitamins and minerals, are also needed to keep our bodies healthy. Together, these substances are called **nutrients**.

Digestion

To release the energy stored in food, our bodies need to break it down. This process is called **digestion**.

thousands of joules in one gram (about 1/30th of an ounce)

total stored chemical energy

energy our bodies can get

fat   carbohydrate   protein

Using the energy in food

When food is digested, the nutrients in it are broken down into tiny parts called molecules. These travel around the body in the **bloodstream**. The nutrients are changed into energy by **chemical reactions**. This energy allows our bodies to work.

The lungs

The chemical reaction that releases energy from food is called **respiration**. This reaction needs oxygen from the air. When we breathe in, oxygen is taken into our bodies by the lungs (above).

nutrient   substance in food that our bodies need to work

Fossil Fuels

Chemical energy is also found stored in **fuels**. The most important fuels are the **fossil fuels**—coal, oil, and natural gas. They are called fossil fuels because they are formed from the remains of living things that died millions of years ago. The **energy** that the plants and animals stored in their bodies is now available for us to use in fossil fuels.

Photosynthesis

Plants (above) make their own food by changing the energy in sunlight into stored chemical energy. This process is called **photosynthesis**.

▼ Coal is an important fuel, but getting it often damages the environment.

fuel   substance that stores energy and releases it when burned

Coal

Coal is formed from the remains of plants that lived 300 million years ago. When these plants died, they formed thick layers that were then covered by mud and sand. The weight of the mud and sand squashed the buried plants. Over millions of years, the plant remains turned into coal.

Digging for coal

Coal near the surface is mined by taking away the soil above it and digging the coal out from beneath. Coal that is buried deep has to be mined from underground. The picture below shows a deep coal mine.

photosynthesis   process by which plants make food using light energy from the Sun

Oil and natural gas

Oil and natural gas were formed in the same way as coal, but from the remains of ancient sea creatures instead of plants.

Oil is a mix of different liquids and chemicals. It can be **refined** and divided into gasoline, diesel, and other **fuels**.

Natural gas is a gas that we use for cooking and heating our houses.

Drilling platforms

Oil and gas are often found deep under the seabed. This large oil and gas platform (below) is drilling out at sea.

refined   cleaned and divided into useful substances

Oil and gas fields

Oil and gas fields are usually found only deep underground. Deep wells have to be drilled through hundreds and hundreds of feet (hundreds of meters) of rock to get to oil and gas fields.

If oil and gas reach the surface, the gas will escape into the air and the oil will form **tar pits**.

▼ "Nodding donkey" pumps are used to pump oil out of the ground.

Burning coal

The **chemical energy** in coal is turned into light and heat **energy** when it is burned.

Nuclear Energy

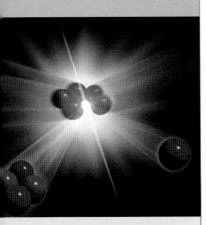

Atomic energy

Energy is given off when the center of an atom, the **nucleus**, is split apart. This picture shows a nucleus being split.

Nuclear **energy** comes from inside **atoms**. When atoms are split apart, energy is released. The nuclear energy can be changed into heat energy that is used to boil water to make steam. The steam turns **turbines** that generate electricity.

The Sun

Another type of nuclear energy is given off by the Sun. Because the Sun is so hot, it causes atoms to join together. This process also gives off huge amounts of energy.

Nuclear power stations

The picture above shows a nuclear **power station**. Nuclear power stations provide 17 percent of the world's electricity.

◀ The Sun gives out huge amounts of heat and light energy.

Losing Energy

Every time an **energy** transfer happens, some energy is lost. Not all of the energy is changed to the type we want.

An electric light bulb changes electrical energy into light energy. However, most of the energy is released as heat, and the bulb gets hot. This is wasted energy. Wasted energy uses up **fossil fuels**, wastes money, and creates more **pollution** than necessary.

Adding up

Energy cannot be created or destroyed. The amount of energy going into a light bulb is the same as the energy coming out. The diagram below shows the huge amount of wasted heat energy and the tiny bit of light energy that comes out of a light bulb.

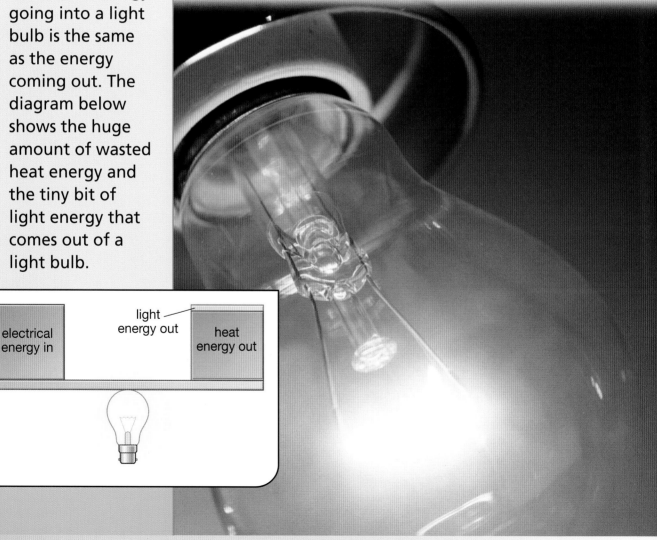

electrical energy in

light energy out

heat energy out

Other wasted energy

Heat energy is the most common type of wasted energy. However, it is not the only type. Sound energy and light energy are often wasted too. When you ride a bike, the stored energy in your body is turned into **kinetic energy** as the wheels go round. If the bike has a rusty chain, some of this energy will be wasted as sound energy when the chain squeaks. Electric fires change electrical energy into heat energy, but they also make wasted light energy.

Computer energy

Computers give out a lot of unwanted heat energy. The picture below shows which areas of the computer are cold (blue) and which are hot (red).

Energy efficiency

We can save **energy** by using more **efficient** equipment. An efficient person is someone who is good at doing his or her job without wasting time or energy. An efficient piece of equipment changes most energy into useful energy and wastes little energy. But no machine can change all the energy it gets into one useful type of energy. Some energy is always wasted.

Efficient light bulbs

In a light bulb, a thin coil of wire gets very hot. This means it glows brightly. This light energy is what we see coming from a light bulb. But the wire also heats up to about 5500°F (3000°C). A lot of heat is given out, which is wasted energy.

An energy-efficient light bulb (below) gives out much less heat than a standard light bulb. It therefore uses much less electricity.

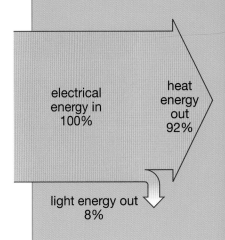

electrical energy in 100%

heat energy out 92%

light energy out 8%

Sankey diagrams

Sankey diagrams are used to show energy changes. The diagram above shows the energy changes in a light bulb. Most of the energy that enters the bulb is changed into heat energy. Only a tiny amount is changed into light.

Moving heat

There are three ways that heat **energy** can move from place to place. These are called radiation, convection, and **conduction**.

Radiation

Infrared radiation is a type of invisible heat energy. All things give off infrared radiation. Hot objects give off more infrared radiation than cold ones. Infrared radiation can travel through air and space. The heat we feel from the Sun is infrared radiation.

Protection from heat

Firefighters (right) wear shiny suits to shield them from the fierce heat of fires.

particle tiny piece of a substance

Convection

When liquids or gases warm up, they **expand**. This makes them lighter and they rise up. When the liquid or gas cools down, it **contracts** and sinks back down.

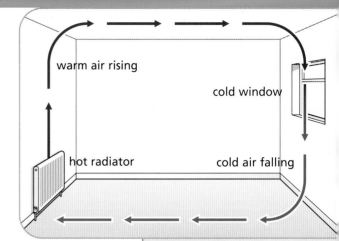

warm air rising

cold window

hot radiator

cold air falling

Conduction

Conduction works best in solids. When the **particles** in a solid are heated, they move or **vibrate** faster. They bump into each other and pass their heat energy on to other particles. The heat is moved through the solid and the solid becomes hotter.

Convection currents

This diagram shows how air moves around a room. The air above the hot radiator is heated and rises. The air near the window is cooler and falls.

◄ The colored blobs of liquid in lava lamps move up and down because of convection.

vibrate   move to and fro

Insulators and conductors

Some things let heat travel through them easily, while others do not. Substances that let heat travel through them are called **conductors**. Metals are good conductors. Substances that do not conduct heat well are called **insulators**.

Double glazing

Houses lose a lot of heat through their windows. Many houses now have insulating glass installed. This uses two layers of glass with a layer of air between them. Air is a good insulator. It slows down the amount of heat lost.

Insulating houses

Houses need to be kept warm in winter and cool in summer. This can be done by insulating the walls and roof space (above). Insulating material has lots of trapped air, which is a poor conductor of heat.

insulator   substance that does not conduct heat or electricity well

Keeping warm in winter

One of the best ways to keep warm in winter is to be well insulated. Animals in cold places have thick layers of fat, feathers, or fur to keep warm. They are all good insulators and reduce heat loss.

Humans need to wrap themselves up in warm clothes to keep their bodies warm. The clothes trap a layer of warm air near their bodies.

Thermoses

A thermos keeps the heat in hot drinks. Inside the thermos are two glass or metal containers, one inside the other. In between the layers is a **vacuum**. Heat cannot be conducted through a vacuum.

▲ Penguins have thick layers of fat and feathers to keep them warm. They also huddle together to share warmth.

Electricity

Balloon electricity

You can see static electricity using a balloon. Rub the balloon on a woolen sweater a few times. This will make the balloon electrically charged. Now hold the balloon over your hair. Your hair will become charged as well and will be attracted to the balloon and rise.

Electricity is a form of **energy**. The type of electrical energy we most often use is called **current electricity**. Tiny, charged **particles** called **electrons** flow through a wire in the same sort of way that water flows through a pipe. Electrons can move through the wire easily because metals are good **conductors** of electricity.

▲ Static electricity causes a spark if it jumps from one object to another.

electron   tiny, negatively-charged particle found in atoms

Static electricity

If electrons move from one object to another, both objects become **electrically charged**. This charge is called **static electricity**. Static electricity is what gives you a small electric shock when you touch something metal after walking on a nylon carpet.

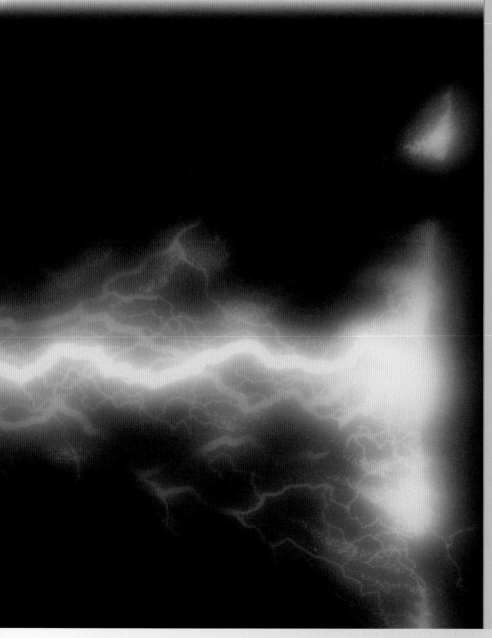

Magnetism

Metals that are **attracted** to a magnet are said to be magnetic. A magnet attracts some metals but not others. A magnet has two ends called the north pole and the south pole. A north pole is always attracted to a south pole, but it is pushed away from another north pole.

Magnetic Earth

Earth is a giant magnet. If you let a magnet swing freely, it will line up so that it is pointing to Earth's magnetic north pole. This is how a compass (right) works. It lets you know in which direction north is.

generator   machine used to make electricity

Electromagnets

In 1819, a scientist discovered that a wire carrying an electric current makes a **magnetic field**. He coiled a lot of wire around a piece of iron and passed electricity through it. This made a powerful magnetic field. He had made an **electromagnet**, a magnet that works using electricity.

Making electricity

In 1831, Michael Faraday found that electricity could be made using magnets. When he moved a magnet near a coil of wire, he found that electricity flowed through the wire. Faraday made the world's first electricity **generator**.

Lightning
Lightning (above) is caused by powerful **static electricity** formed in clouds during thunderstorms.

◄ Strong electromagnets are used to pick up iron and steel in scrap yards. They can be switched on to pick up materials, and off to drop them again.

Turbines

A turbine (below) is a bit like a windmill with many blades. The blades are turned by fast-moving steam. This movement energy can be turned into electricity.

Power stations

Electricity is made in **power stations**. Power stations change the stored energy in **fuels** into movement or **kinetic energy**. When fuels are burned, their stored **chemical energy** is turned into heat **energy**. The heat is used to boil water. Steam from the boiling water is used to turn **turbines**, which turn **generators**. These generate electricity.

Hydroelectric power

Moving water is also a major source of energy. At a **hydroelectric power** station, a river is dammed to make a lake. The lake is a source of stored energy. When the water is allowed to flow, the kinetic energy in the water turns the turbines. The turbines are attached to electricity generators. Energy from the water makes the electricity generators run.

Electricity can also be generated from the energy in the **tides** and from wave power.

▼ This power station burns coal.

Energy transfer diagrams

Energy transfer diagrams show how energy is moved along from one place to another. This diagram shows how the energy is transferred in a coalfired power station.

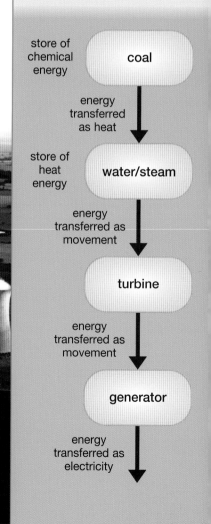

store of chemical energy — coal

energy transferred as heat

store of heat energy — water/steam

energy transferred as movement

turbine

energy transferred as movement

generator

energy transferred as electricity

---

tide   daily movement of water in the seas and oceans

Sound Energy

Sound is a form of **energy** that we can hear. When an object moves, it **vibrates**. The vibrations make a sound wave. We usually hear sound waves that are passed through the air, but sound can also travel through solids and liquids.

Pitch

The **pitch** of a sound is how high or low it is. Children usually have higher voices than adults. Their voices have a higher pitch.

▼ Ear defenders protect the ears from being damaged by very loud sounds.

Microphones

Microphones change sound energy into electrical energy. When you speak into a microphone, the sound energy from your voice makes a disk called a **diaphragm** vibrate. The vibrations are then changed into electrical energy.

Loudspeakers

Loudspeakers change electrical energy into sound energy. The electrical energy causes the diaphragm to vibrate, which makes sound waves. When you turn the volume of your television up, you are making the vibrations of the diaphragm larger.

▼ This loudspeaker has been cut away so you can see inside it.

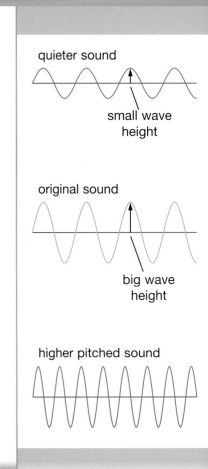

quieter sound

small wave height

original sound

big wave height

higher pitched sound

Seeing waves

There is a machine that can show the pattern of a sound on a screen. The diagrams above show the vibrations in a sound wave from three different sounds.

Hearing sounds

Our ears pick up sound **energy** from the air around us. This is turned into electrical **signals** that are carried to our brain. The brain then works out what sound we are hearing. Having two ears helps us tell which direction a sound is coming from. Some animals have very large ears so that they can hear the quietest of sounds.

Inside the ear

Part of your ear contains tiny hairs (above), which **vibrate** when sound energy is passed to them. The hairs send signals to your brain, which tells you what you are hearing.

▼ Bats use echoes from ultrasound squeaks to find insects to eat.

Ultrasound

Sounds that have a very high **pitch** are called **ultrasound**. We cannot hear ultrasound because it is outside the range of human hearing. Bats can make and hear ultrasound noises. The sounds they make bounce off objects and back into their ears. This is called **echolocation**.

When sound waves hit an object, some of the energy is **reflected** back, making an **echo**. Submarines use sonar, a type of echolocation, to find objects underwater.

Ultrasound scans

Ultrasound scans are a safe way of checking how an unborn baby is growing.
A machine sends out ultrasound waves that are bounced off the baby. A computer uses the echoes to make a picture of the baby. Doctors can clearly see the baby (left).

echo   sound that has bounced back off a surface

Many Changes

Clockwork radios

In 1993, an English engineer invented a clockwork radio like the one in the picture below. By turning a handle, you wound up a spring in the radio. The **kinetic energy** from turning the handle is stored in the spring as **elastic energy**. When the radio is turned on, the spring slowly unwinds. It changes the stored elastic **energy** back into kinetic energy. This turns a small **generator** that makes the electricity the radio needs to work.

Electronic watches

Electronic watches have a tiny, **vibrating** crystal inside them (below). These watches keep much better time than clockwork ones.

Word Store   kinetic energy   energy of all moving things

Northern lights

Have you heard of the northern or southern lights? These are the colorful swirling patterns of light that we can sometimes see over the North or South Pole.

These amazing lights are caused by a very fast **solar wind**. When the solar wind meets Earth's **magnetic field,** the **energy** from the wind is turned into light energy by gases in the **atmosphere.**

▼ The polar lights sometimes shine in the skies at night.

solar wind   tiny particles coming off the Sun into space

Wasted heat

When **fuels** are burned in **power stations**, huge amounts of heat are given off. Some of this is trapped and used to generate electricity, but much is lost into the **atmosphere**. These cooling towers show heat escaping in **water vapor**.

The Big Bang

Scientists are not certain exactly how the **universe** began, but most believe it started with the Big Bang.

About 14 billion years ago, the universe started as something very small and very hot. It then got very big very quickly and started cooling down. Its starting temperature was probably about 250 million times hotter than boiling water. The average temperature of the universe today is $-454.7°F$ ($-270.4°C$.)

Where has all this heat **energy** gone?

Changing energy

The heat energy from the beginning of the universe has not gone. It has just been changed into other types of energy. As the early universe got bigger, all the stars and **galaxies** were created from the **matter** and energy within it.

The universe is still getting bigger. It will probably do this for at least another 10 billion years and may even go on forever.

End of the Sun

The Sun has enough hydrogen fuel left to shine for another 4.5 billion years. After this, the Sun will become a giant red star. After another half-billion years, the Sun will shrink and become a cold, white dwarf star.

galaxy   a huge group of stars that covers billions of miles of space

Find Out More

Organizations

Energy Quest

Energy Quest is the award-winning energy education web site of the California Energy Commission. Contact them at the following address:

Energy Quest
California Energy Commission
Media and Public Communications Office
1516 Ninth Street, MS-29
Sacramento, CA 95814-5504

Books

Oxlade, Chris. *Energy (Science Topics)*. Chicago: Heinemann Library, 1999.

Parker, Steve. *Science Files: Energy (series)*. Milwaukee: Gareth Stevens, 2004.

Saunders, Nigel, and Steven Chapman. *Fossil Fuel (Energy Essentials)*. Chicago: Raintree, 2005.

World Wide Web

To find out more about energy transfers, you can search the Internet using keywords like these:

- "kinetic energy"
- energy +transfer
- light +energy"
- gravitational +energy
- sound +energy
- elastic +energy
- nuclear +energy
- potential +energy

You can find your own keywords by using words from this book. The search tips opposite will help you find the most useful web sites.

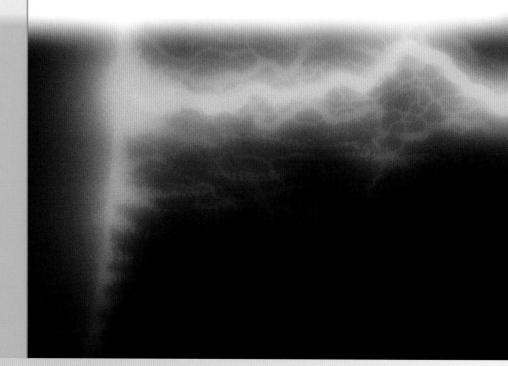

Search tips

There are billions of pages on the Internet. It can be difficult to find exactly what you are looking for. These tips will help you find useful web sites more quickly:

- Know what you want to find out about.
- Use simple keywords.
- Use two to six keywords in a search.
- Only use names of people, places, or things.
- Put double quotation marks around words that go together, for example, "sound energy" or "energy transfer"

Where to search

Search engine

A search engine looks through millions of web site pages. It lists all the sites that match the words in the search box. You will find that the best matches are at the top of the list, on the first page.

Search directory

A person instead of a computer has sorted a search directory. You can search by keyword or subject and browse through the different sites. It is like looking through books on a library shelf.

Glossary

atmosphere layer of gases surrounding Earth

atom smallest bit of a substance

attracted drawn towards

bloodstream network of blood vessels in the body

bond force that sticks atoms together

chemical energy energy that is released during chemical reactions

chemical reaction when changes happen to a substance

conduction transfer of heat through a substance; heat always moves from an area of higher temperature to an area of lower temperature

conductor substance that conducts heat or electricity

contract get smaller

current electricity electricity formed when electric charges move

cylinder moving part in an engine

diaphragm vibrating disk in a microphone, loudspeaker, or ear

digestion breaking food down into smaller bits

echo sound that has bounced back off a surface

echolocation using echoes to find objects

efficient good at doing its job without wasting energy

elastic energy energy stored when something is stretched, squashed, or bent

electrically charged given a charge, or bit of, electrical energy, either positive or negative

electromagnet magnet that works using electricity

electron tiny, negatively-charged particle found in atoms

energy being able to do work. Light, heat, and electricity are types of energy.

expand get bigger

flywheel heavy spinning wheel

force push or pull

fossil fuel fuel formed from the remains of ancient plants and animals

fuel substance that stores energy and releases it when burned

galaxy a huge group of stars that covers billions of miles of space

generator machine used to make electricity

gravity force that pulls everything together and keeps us on the ground

gravitational energy energy stored when something is lifted up

hydroelectric power electricity made by using moving water

infrared radiation invisible heat energy

insulator substance that does not conduct heat or electricity very well

joule unit of energy

kinetic energy energy of moving things

magnetic field space around a magnet

where magnetic power can be felt

matter anything that has mass and takes up space

microphone device that changes sound energy into electrical energy

nucleus center of an atom

nutrient substance in food that our bodies need to work

particle tiny piece of a substance

photosynthesis process by which plants make food using light energy from the Sun

pitch how high or low a sound it

pollution harmful substances in the air, water, or on land

power station place where electricity is generated

refined cleaned and divided into useful substances

reflected bounced

respiration chemical reaction that releases energy from food

rim outer edge of a wheel or flywheel

signals signs or messages

solar wind tiny particles coming off the Sun into space

static electricity effect when electric charges stay still in one place

tar pits pools of oil on the surface of the ground

tides daily movement of water in the seas and oceans

turbine machinery that is turned by water, steam, gas, or air

ultrasound sound with a very high

frequency

universe everything that exists on Earth and in space

vacuum empty space with nothing in it, not even air

vibrate move to and fro

water vapor water in the form of a gas

Index